DRAW COMIC STRIPS

WITH AJIT NARAYAN

SCHOLASTIC
New York Toronto London Auckland
Sydney New Delhi Hong Kong

This edition is dedicated to my wife Liji & daughter Alankrita

Published by Scholastic India Pvt. Ltd.
A subsidiary of Scholastic Inc., New York, 10012 (USA).
Publishers since 1920, with international operations in Canada, Australia, New Zealand, the United Kingdom, India, and Hong Kong.

For information regarding permission, write to:
Scholastic India Pvt. Ltd.
A-27, Ground Floor, Bharti Sigma Centre,
Infocity-I, Sector-34, Gurgaon 122001 (India).

First edition: May 2013
This reprint edition February 2026

ISBN-13: 978-93-5103-006-5

Printed at Shivam Offset Press, New Delhi

CONTENTS

ABOUT THE AUTHOR

PROFESSIONAL CARTOONIST AND WORKSHOP CONSULTANT, AJIT NARAYAN HAS BEEN DRAWING AND ILLUSTRATING FOR OVER 20 YEARS. THE BOOKS HE HAS AUTHORED INCLUDE **CARTOONING WITH AJIT NARAYAN, HOW TO DRAW ANIMAL CARTOONS** AND **DRAW CARTOONS WITH AJIT NARAYAN.**

INTRODUCTION

CREATING COMIC STRIPS IS A FORM OF CARTOONING THAT BELONGS TO A DIFFERENT WORLD, WITH ITS OWN SET OF RULES AND TECHNIQUES. IT IS A CREATIVE PROCESS INVOLVING NOT JUST YOUR DRAWING SKILLS, BUT ALSO YOUR ABILITY TO WRITE, DIRECT AND ACT.

THIS ONE-STOP GUIDE BOOK IS THE PLACE TO START, TO KNOW HOW IT IS DONE!

COMIC STRIPS

A SERIES OF DRAWINGS MADE IN A SEQUENCE AND PLACED ADJACENT TO EACH OTHER WITHIN BOXES, PANELS OR FRAMES IS KNOWN AS A COMIC STRIP.

IT IS IMPORTANT TO UNDERSTAND HOW THE STRIP CAN BE MADE APPEALING AND HOW THE CHARACTERS CAN BE BROUGHT TO LIFE.

LET US BEGIN WITH THE BASIC COMIC STRIP LAYOUT, WHICH USUALLY HAS THREE TO FOUR PANELS.

BASIC 4-PANEL COMIC STRIP LAYOUT

SETTING SITUATION REACTION OUTCOME

SETTING (INTRODUCTORY PANEL)

DRAW THE START OF THE STORY OR JOKE.

USING MULTIPLE PANELS ALLOWS A LITTLE MORE DEPTH. THE FIRST PANEL NORMALLY ILLUSTRATES THE CONCEPT OR SETTING.

SITUATION—REACTION (DEVELOPING THE JOKE)

DRAW THE MIDDLE OF YOUR STORY OR JOKE.

THE SECOND PANEL SETS UP THE SITUATION AND INTERACTION BETWEEN A COUPLE OF CHARACTERS, SOMETHING HAPPENING TO SOMEONE, ETC. THE THIRD PANEL IS USED TO RESOLVE SOMETHING OR A REACTION.

OUTCOME (PUNCHLINE)

DRAW THE END OF YOUR STORY OR JOKE.

FINALLY, YOU SHOW THE OUTCOME OF THE SITUATION.

TYPES OF COMIC STRIPS

THE ***DAILY STRIP***, IS PROBABLY THE SIMPLEST FORM OF COMIC STRIP. SEEN MOSTLY IN NEWSPAPERS, IT SIMPLY LETS THE CONVERSATION BETWEEN CHARACTERS UNFOLD AND ALLOWS THE READERS TO PEEP INTO THEIR WORLD. THE BACKGROUND MAY ONLY BE SUGGESTED IN MOST CASES OR BE ABSENT ALTOGETHER.

AS LONG AS THE DRAWINGS ARE SIMPLE, THE CARTOONIST CAN BE SURE THAT THE READER WILL NOT LOSE SIGHT OF THE REAL MOTIVE BEHIND THE DRAWING—THE TELLING OF A JOKE. HAVING MULTIPLE PANELS ALLOWS YOU TO BUILD UP THE JOKE, TAKING INTO ACCOUNT THE TIME FACTOR, WITH THE PUNCHLINE BEING DELIVERED IN THE LAST PANEL. THIS APPROACH IS THE CLOSEST TO THE WAY A JOKE IS TOLD ALL OVER THE WORLD. THREE TO FOUR PANELS LEND YOU THE OPPORTUNITY TO CREATE SUSPENSE, DELIVER THE PUNCHLINE, AND FINALLY RELEASE THE TENSION TO INVITE LAUGHTER.

THE OTHER FORMAT IS THE **COMIC BOOK** OR CONTINUITY STRIP. THESE ARE USED IN ADVENTURE OR NARRATIVE STORIES, WHERE MANY TRICKS CAN BE EMPLOYED TO LET THE READER KNOW OF THE PASSAGE OF TIME. IF YOU CHOOSE CONTINUITY STRIPS, YOU NEED TO NOT ONLY POSSESS SOME STORYTELLING SKILLS BUT ALSO KNOW HOW TO KEEP THE STORY FROM LOSING ITS APPEAL. THE READERS SHOULD NOT AT ANY POINT FIND THE STORY DULL.

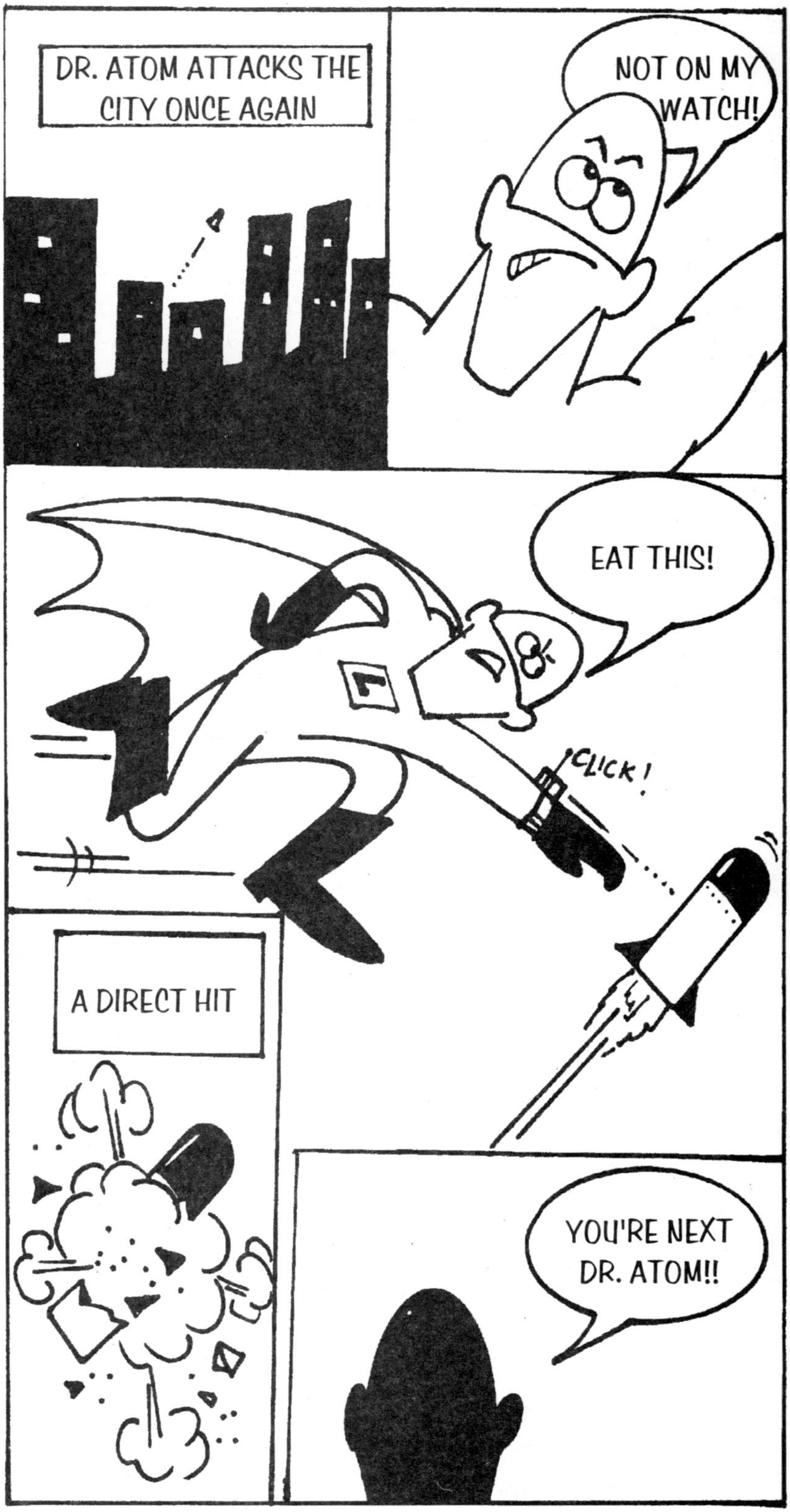

A COMIC BOOK PAGE AS A WHOLE, SHOULD READ LIKE A SENTENCE. BEGINNING FROM THE UPPER LEFT CORNER, THE ACTION FLOWS ACROSS THE PAGE TO THE RIGHT, MOVING DOWN TO THE LEFT HAND CORNER AND THEN TO THE BOTTOM RIGHT, IN A ZIGZAG PATTERN.

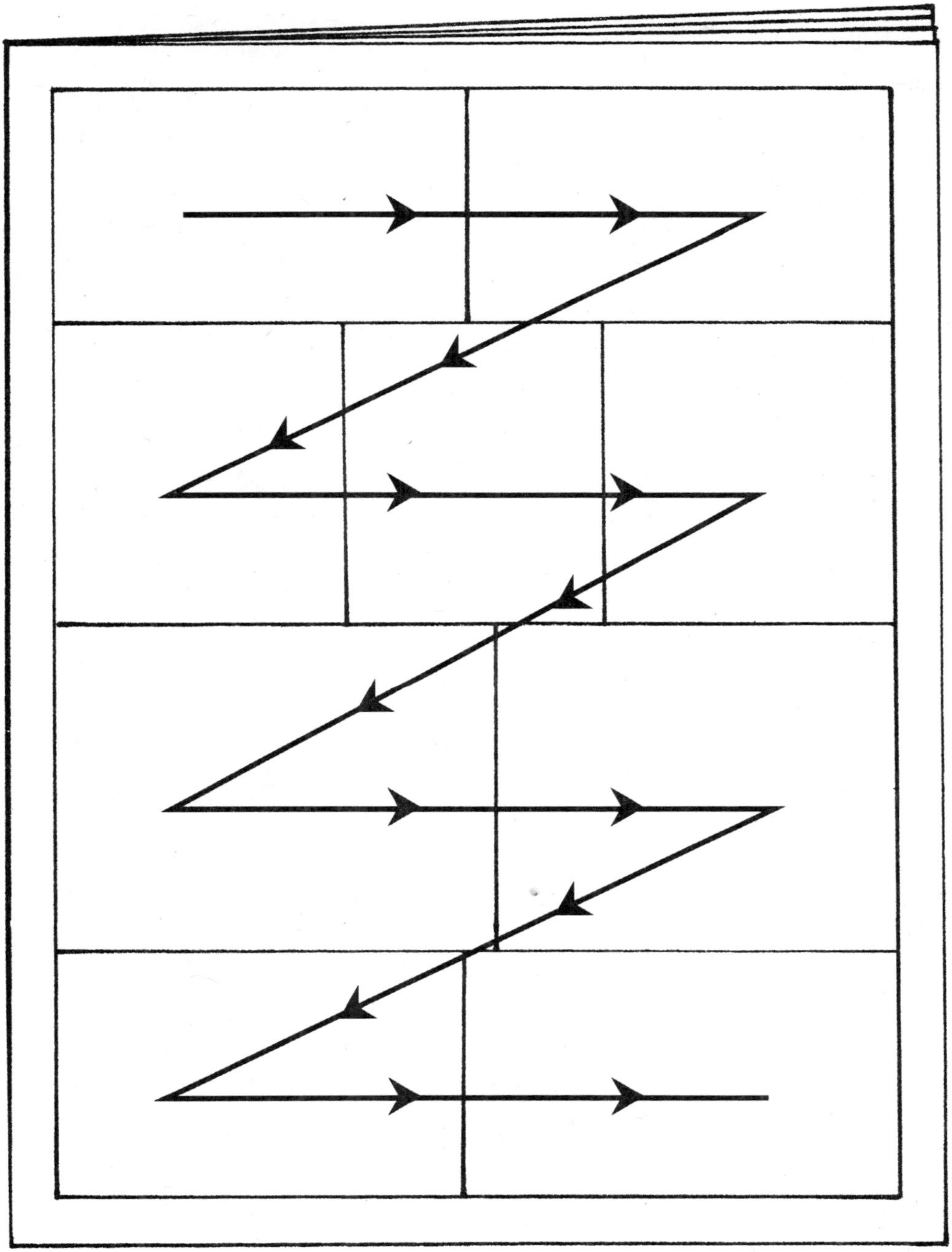

THE THIRD FORMAT IS THE 'JOKE A DAY' STRIP, ALSO CALLED THE ***SINGLE PANEL STRIP***. THIS IS A TOUGH FORMAT BECAUSE YOU NEED TO CONSTANTLY THINK OF COMIC ONE-LINERS OR JOKES BASED ON CURRENT AFFAIRS, CELEBRITIES OR RECOUNT INTERESTING OBSERVATION.

NO MORE CARTOON CHANNEL. YOU'VE GOT A **CARTOON EYE** INFECTION!

WHAT DISTINGUISHES A CONTINUITY STRIP FROM A DAILY AND SINGLE-GAG CARTOON IS THAT IT INCLUDES THE ELEMENT OF TIME.

IN THIS BOOK, WE WILL BE FOCUSING ON THE FIRST FORMAT ONLY, WHICH IS THE SIMPLEST TO CREATE.

IDEA

BEFORE YOU BEGIN, YOU NEED TO HAVE AN IDEA OR A THEME TO BASE YOUR DRAWINGS ON. THE STEPS TO FOLLOW ARE

1. RESEARCH

YOU HAVE TO GET FAMILIAR WITH POPULAR COMIC STRIPS THAT ALREADY EXIST. THOUGH YOU ARE OBVIOUSLY NOT EXPECTED TO HAVE EVERY SINGLE SERIES THAT HAS EVER BEEN PRODUCED AT YOUR FINGERTIPS, IT WILL SUFFICE TO BE AWARE OF THE WELL-KNOWN NAMES IN THIS FIELD OF ART AND THE LATEST TRENDS IN COMICS. THIS WILL KEEP YOU FROM GLORIFYING YOUR OWN IDEA AS AN ORIGINAL WHILE IT MAY ACTUALLY BE QUITE A COMMON ONE IN THE FIELD.

2. GENERATING NEW IDEAS

DURING YOUR RESEARCH, YOU MAY CHANCE UPON SOME IDEAS THAT COULD BE USED TO COME UP WITH A TOTALLY NEW CONCEPT. ALL YOU MIGHT NEED TO DO IS GIVE IT A NEW ANGLE. YOU COULD ALSO COMBINE TWO IDEAS TO FORM A BRAND NEW ONE.

3. EXPERIMENT

REMEMBER, NOT ALL IDEAS ARE BRILLIANT. SOME MAY EVEN SEEM REALLY NAIVE INITIALLY. BUT DON'T GIVE UP. THESE IDEAS MAY FORM THE BASIS OF YOUR NEW COMIC STRIP. PLAY WITH THEM IN YOUR MIND, MIX THEM, STIR THEM, JUGGLE WITH KNOWN DRAWING TECHNIQUES AND FINALLY COME UP WITH YOUR OWN ORIGINAL STYLE. THE MORE YOU DO THIS, THE MORE ARE YOUR CHANCES OF CREATING SOMETHING NOVEL.

WATT is best?!

4. CHOICE

ONCE YOU HAVE SHORT-LISTED YOUR IDEAS, YOU HAVE TO SELECT THE BEST ONE. YOUR READERS SHOULD GET NOTHING BUT THE BEST PERSPECTIVE. YOUR CREATION SHOULD BE NOTHING BUT ORIGINAL. REMEMBER, ORIGINAL IDEAS NEVER FAIL TO APPEAL.

5. TESTING YOUR IDEAS

MAKE ROUGH SKETCHES BASED ON YOUR IDEAS. PRESENT THEM TO FRIENDS, FAMILY MEMBERS OR PEOPLE WHOSE OPINIONS YOU TRUST. IT WOULD BE BETTER IF THESE PEOPLE HAVE NO IDEA OF THIS ART FORM. THEIR REACTIONS AND COMMENTS WILL HELP YOU FINALISE YOUR SELECTION. REMEMBER, WHAT YOU THINK IS A GREAT AND ORIGINAL IDEA MAY ACTUALLY NOT APPEAR SO TO OTHERS.

THESE FIVE STEPS WILL HELP YOU CHOOSE THE RIGHT COMIC STRIP IDEA. JUST MAKE SURE YOU ENJOY EACH STAGE OF THE CREATIVE PROCESS.

YOU NEED A THEME, SUBJECT OR SITUATION TO BEGIN WORK ON THE COMIC STRIP WITH. BUT YOU HAVE TO COME UP WITH A STORY. FALL BACK ON WHAT YOU HAVE READ IN BOOKS, MAGAZINES OR NOVELS. RECALL FILMS, INCIDENTS OR EVENTS YOU HAVE SEEN OR WITNESSED. BROWSE THE INTERNET, GO THROUGH OLD MAGAZINES. YOU WILL BE AMAZED AT THE IDEAS YOU GET WHILE DOING SO. THINKING OF EVENTS, INCIDENTS OR THINGS THAT ANNOY YOU CAN ALSO GIVE YOU GREAT IDEAS.

YOUR IDEAS COULD BE BASED ON ANY OF THE FOLLOWING

1. **PERSONAL EXPERIENCE:** THINK OF SOME RECENT INCIDENT THAT MADE YOU LAUGH, EXPERIENCES THAT YOU HAVE HAD WITH YOUR PEERS, CHILDREN, PETS.

2. **PUN:** USE ONE-LINERS, CLEVER REMARKS OR WITTY COMMENTS BASED ON ONE WORD OR PHRASE SOUNDING LIKE ANOTHER.

3. **PAIRING:** TWO CONFLICTING ELEMENTS CAN BE COMBINED TO CREATE A HUMOROUS SITUATION.

4. **HISTORY:** RECALL SOME HISTORICAL EVENT OR CHARACTER THAT CAN BE PLACED IN AN AMUSING SITUATION CONTRARY TO THEIR ORIGINAL BACKGROUND.

5. **ANTHROPOMORPHISM:** IT IS THE MOST POPULAR TECHNIQUE USED BY CARTOONISTS WORLDWIDE, THROUGH WHICH HUMAN QUALITIES ARE ATTRIBUTED TO ANIMALS OR INANIMATE OBJECTS, CREATING SCOPE FOR HUMOUR.

6. **VISUAL:** VISUALISE A REALLY WEIRD OR RIDICULOUS IMAGE WITH A FUNNY PUNCHLINE ATTACHED TO IT. EVEN WITHOUT A PUNCHLINE, SOMETIMES THE SILLINESS OF THE IMAGE IS ENOUGH TO MAKE IT COMICAL.

STORY AND CHARACTERISATION

THOUGH THE ULTIMATE AIM IS TO DRAW THE ATTENTION OF YOUR READERS, YOU HAVE TO ENSURE THAT THEIR INTEREST IS SUSTAINED TILL THE END. THEREFORE, MAKE SURE THAT YOUR STORY HAS THE FOLLOWING:

1. AN INTERESTING BEGINNING

2. AN EXCITING ENDING

REMEMBER, NOT ALL COMIC STRIPS ARE MEANT TO BE FUNNY.

DO NOT COPY AN EXISTING IDEA OR STRIP. IF YOUR THEME IS SIMILAR, MAKE SURE THAT THE PERSPECTIVE IS NEW.

TIP: IF YOU HAVE AN IDEA FOR A DRAMATIC OR FUNNY ENDING, YOU CAN WORK BACKWARDS—FROM THE CLIMAX TO THE BEGINNING.

RULES FOR DIALOGUE WRITING

1. DON'T FORCE UNNECESSARY WORDS ON YOUR READERS.
2. KEEP SENTENCES SHORT AND END THE DIALOGUES BEFORE THEY LOSE THEIR PUNCH.
3. A STANDARD CARTOON TECHNIQUE IS NOT TO RESPOND DIRECTLY TO WHAT IS BEING SAID.
4. THINK OF SILLY QUESTIONS YOUR CHARACTERS MIGHT ASK AND THE SILLY ANSWERS THEY MIGHT BE GIVEN.
5. IMAGINE YOUR CHARACTERS IN AMUSING BUT UNUSUAL SITUATIONS. HERE ARE SOME EXAMPLES, YOU MUST KEEP ADDING TO THIS LIST:

CHARACTERS	SITUATIONS
CAVEMAN	READING NEWSPAPER
SPACE ALIEN	EATING A PIZZA
ANCIENT EGYPTIANS	VISITING A MUSEUM
SKELETON	DREAMING
MAN-EATING PLANT	EATING A BANANA
FLY	WATCHING TV
BABY	TEXTING ON A CELLPHONE
COW	DRIVING A TRACTOR
DOG	WORKING ON A COMPUTER
SCIENTIST	PLAYING A VIDEO GAME

TIP :
DO NOT FORCE YOUR IDEAS. IF YOU FEEL THAT A CERTAIN IDEA IS NOT WORKING, JUST DROP IT AND GO ON TO SOMETHING NEW.

CHARACTERISATION

WHEN IT COMES TO DESIGNING CHARACTERS, THE MOST VALUABLE TOOL FOR A COMIC ARTIST IS THE POWER OF OBSERVATION. YOU WILL FIND THAT THE BEST COMICS/ FICTIONAL CHARACTERS ARE USUALLY BASED ON PEOPLE AND PETS THAT THE ARTIST SEES AROUND HIM. REMEMBER, CHARACTERS CAN ONLY BE BELIEVABLE IF THEY DISPLAY REAL EMOTIONS AND TEMPERAMENTS. ONE CHARACTER COULD ALSO BE SHOWN TO POSSESS TWO CONTRADICTORY CHARACTERISTICS.

YOU COULD DECIDE ON EITHER A SINGLE CENTRAL CHARACTER OR TWO. WHILE DESIGNING YOUR CHARACTER, MAKE SURE YOU GIVE IT A PROMINENT FEATURE THAT CAN BE RECOGNISED WHETHER HE IS UP CLOSE, IN THE BACKGROUND OR A SILHOUETTE.

THE CHARACTERS MUST BE RELATABLE, WITH FEATURES AND CLOTHING REFLECTING THEIR PERSONALITY. SO, BASE THEM ON SOMEONE YOU KNOW, EVEN BETTER, YOUR OWN SELF! MAKE DRAWINGS OF YOUR CHARACTER'S HEAD FROM THE FRONT, SIDE, REAR ETC.

TO SHOW YOUR CHARACTERS FROM DIFFERENT ANGLES, MAKE SURE YOU HAVE A **MODEL SHEET** FOR EACH ONE OF THEM.

YOU DO NOT NEED TO GIVE HIM TOO MANY DETAILS SINCE THE DRAWING WILL BE QUITE SMALL ANYWAY.

THE ARTIST SHOULD HAVE ALL THE ADDITIONAL DETAILS OF THE CHARACTER'S FEATURES, ATTIRE, LOCATIONS FOR READY REFERENCE SO THAT THE STORY DOESN'T MEET WITH ANY BUMPS.

TO ASSEMBLE A CAST, THE MAIN CHARACTER NEEDS TO BE SUPPORTED BY SEVERAL MINOR CHARACTERS. THE THREE TYPES OF CHARACTERS IN A COMIC STRIP ARE:

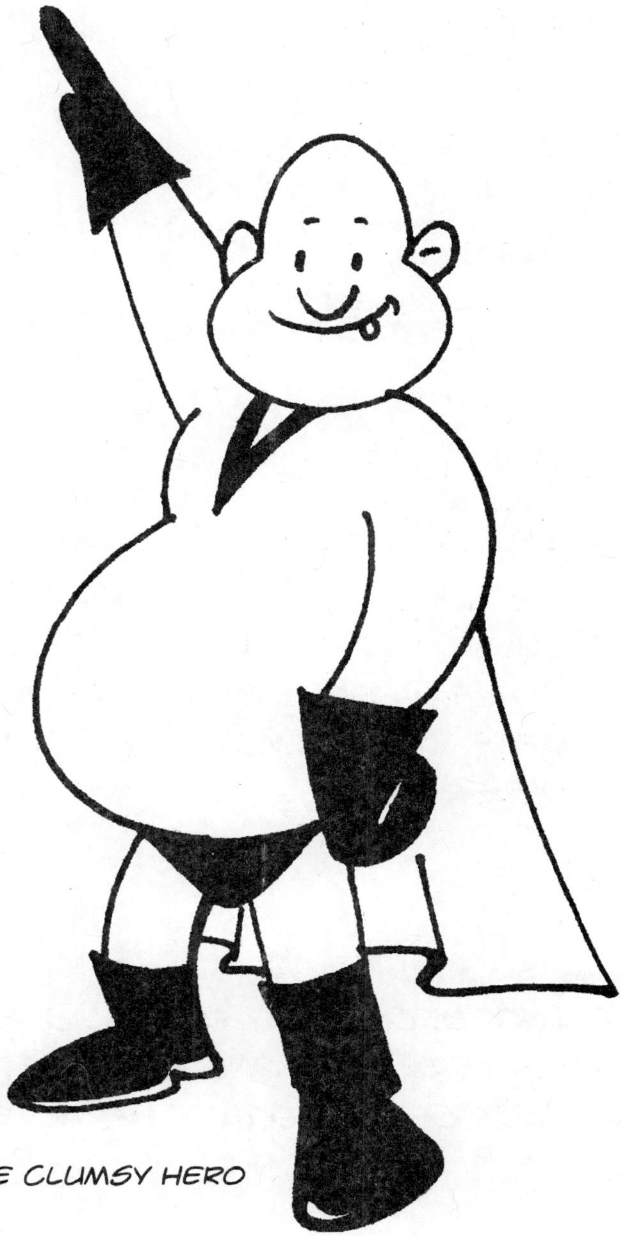

THE CLUMSY HERO

MAIN / CENTRAL

THE CENTRAL CHARACTER APPEARS REGULARLY IN THE COMIC STRIP, FOR EXAMPLE, THE CLUMSY HERO.

HERO'S
FAITHFUL DOG

SUPPORTING

THESE CHARACTERS APPEAR LESS FREQUENTLY IN THE COMIC STRIP, FOR EXAMPLE, THE CLUMSY HERO'S DOG.

ANCILLARY

THESE CHARACTERS ARE THE LEAST FREQUENT, YET NEVER FORGOTTEN, FOR EXAMPLE, THE CLUMSY HERO'S GRANDPA.

HERO'S
GRANDPA

TIP:

IT IS NOT NECESSARY FOR ALL STRIPS TO HAVE A FIXED SET OF CHARACTERS. AS LONG AS YOUR THEME IS CONSISTENT, YOU CAN KEEP CHANGING THE CHARACTERS IF YOU NEED TO.

SCRIPT TO STRIP

ONCE YOU HAVE COMPLETED THE TEXT PART OF YOUR STRIP, YOU CAN BEGIN DRAWING SMALL, FREEHAND SKETCHES.

ONCE YOU HAVE MADE A PENCIL SKETCH, YOU WILL GET A BETTER IDEA OF THE LAYOUT. NEXT, TAKE ANOTHER PIECE OF PAPER AND USE A RULER TO DRAW YOUR PANELS, KEEPING IN MIND THE SPACE REQUIRED TO ACCOMMODATE SPEECH BALLOONS. YOU CAN THEN WRITE THE DIALOGUES LIGHTLY.

ROUGH SCRIPT

(IT IS JUST A ROUGH DRAFT OF THE JOKE OR STORY.)

MOTHER: Shame on you! You just got 15 out of 40?

SON: Oh, Mom! It could have been much worse.

MOTHER: How?

SON: If I had sat next to Raj I would have got just 10 out of 40.

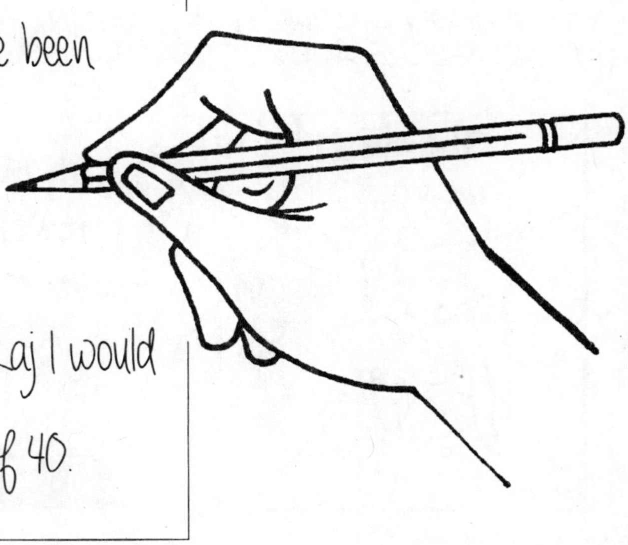

PANEL-BY-PANEL SCRIPT

WITHOUT CROWDING TOO MUCH DIALOGUE INTO ONE FRAME, VISUALISE THE JOKE FRAME BY FRAME.

FRAME 1. A mother is looking at her son's test results. She is sitting across the desk, looking at him.

(MOTHER: Shame on you! You just got 15 out of 40?)

FRAME 2. Son, with a sheepish expression, explains.

(SON: Oh, Mom! It could have been much worse.)

Mother poses a question.

(MOTHER: How?)

FRAME 3. Son, with a casual expression while the mother looks stunned.

(SON: If I had sat next to Raj I would have got just 10 out of 40.)

IN THE FINAL INKED VERSION, SOME CHANGES ARE MADE AND DIALOGUES ARE STREAMLINED.

THUMBNAIL

ONCE AN IDEA STRIKES YOU, MAKE A NOTE OF IT BEFORE IT FADES AWAY. MAKE ROUGH SKETCHES TO DEPICT THE JOKE PANEL BY PANEL.

REMEMBER, THE COMIC STRIP PANEL COMPRISES NOT ONLY THE ACTIONS OF THE CHARACTERS BUT ALSO THEIR DIALOGUE. THE WAY THE DIALOGUE IS WRITTEN WILL DETERMINE THE WAY THE STORY IS DIVIDED INTO PANELS. IT IS BEST TO ARRANGE IT IN SUCH A WAY THAT THERE IS JUST ONE DIALOGUE EXCHANGED PER PANEL. THIS EXCHANGE WILL COMPRISE ONE CHARACTER'S STATEMENT AND THE OTHER CHARACTER'S RESPONSE.

AS A RULE, SPEECH BALLOONS SHOULD NOT CONTAIN MORE THAN 20 WORDS. THEREFORE, A PANEL SHOULD BE LIMITED TO 40 WORDS TO ENSURE THAT THE COMIC STRIP IS NOT TOO 'WORDY'.

THE BEST COMIC STRIPS ARE OFTEN THOSE THAT CONTAIN NO WORDS! SO, DON'T BE AFRAID TO CREATE FRAMES WITHOUT DIALOGUES.

HERE IS THE GENERAL PROCESS OF CREATING A STRIP.

LETTERING FIRST

USE A RULER TO DRAW YOUR GUIDELINES AND PENCIL THE DIALOGUE.

PLAN

VISUALISE THE SCENE, THE DIALOGUE SPACE, THE CAPTIONS, THE SPEECH BALLOONS, EVEN THE ANGLES. THEN, PLAN YOUR FRAMES SO THAT THE STORY FLOWS SMOOTHLY.

INK

AFTER YOU FINISH YOUR PENCIL DRAWINGS, GO OVER THEM WITH AN INK PEN.

STAGING

YOU MAY HAVE TO THINK LIKE A FILM DIRECTOR AND INTERPRET THE VISUAL LANGUAGE OF THE COMIC STRIP, WITH VARYING FRAMES AND EXCITING CAMERA ANGLES.

LET US LOOK AT THE STEPS IN A STANDARD STAGING PROCESS.

LONG SHOT | MEDIUM SHOT | CLOSE UP | WIDE SHOT

STEP 1

BEGIN BY ESTABLISHING THE LOCATION **(LONG SHOT)**. MAKE SURE THAT THE READER IS ABLE TO CLEARLY SEE THE CHARACTERS AND THE SETTING.

STEP 2

FOCUS ON THE CHARACTERS AND THE DIALOGUE **(MEDIUM SHOT)**.

STEP 3

HIGHLIGHT THE EMOTION **(CLOSE-UP OR HEAD SHOT)**. THIS IS THE MOST IMPORTANT PANEL OF THE STRIP.

STEP 4

BRING THE ACTION TO A CONCLUSION **(WIDE SHOT)**. THIS IS THE STAGE WHERE YOU CAN RE-ESTABLISH THE LOCATION AND DELIVER THE PUNCHLINE. REMEMBER, THE READER WILL WANT TO SEE HOW THE OTHER CHARACTER REACTS.

SPECIALTY SHOTS

USED ON RARE OCCASIONS TO ADD PUNCH.

EXTREME CLOSE-UP

USED TO DISPLAY FACIAL EXPRESSION AND EMOTIONS AND CREATE A POWERFUL IMPACT.

DETAILED SHOT

USED TO SHOW INTERACTION AND HIGHLIGHT DRAMA.

EXTREME LONG SHOT

USED TO HEIGHTEN DRAMATIC EFFECT WITH HIGH HORIZON LINE.

SILHOUETTE

SILHOUETTES ARE SOMETIMES USED IN THE MIDDLE FRAMES OF COMIC STRIPS WHEN ACTION IS MINIMAL. CREATING SILHOUETTES INVOLVES PRESENTING KNOWN AND IDENTIFIABLE SHAPES OF PEOPLE IN BLACK AND WHITE CONTRASTS.

SILHOUETTES SHOULD NOT BE IDEALLY USED IN THE FIRST AND LAST FRAMES BECAUSE THE READER WILL BE UNABLE TO RECOGNISE WHO THE CHARACTER IS (IN THE FIRST FRAME) AND WHAT HIS REACTION IS (IN THE FINAL FRAME).

SILHOUETTES WORK BEST WHEN THEY ARE USED TO ESTABLISH A MOOD OR IN LONG SHOTS.

MOOD SILHOUETTE

LONG SHOT SILHOUETTE

A POPULAR TECHNIQUE EMPLOYED BY CARTOONISTS IS THE **BLACKOUT FRAME** WHICH LETS READERS IDENTIFY CHARACTERS, EVEN IN TOTAL DARKNESS, BY RECOGNISING THE SHAPES OF THEIR EYES.

DARK HOUSES OR BUILDINGS WITH WHITE (GLOWING) WINDOWS CAN BE USED TO DEPICT A NIGHT SCENE.

SILHOUETTES WORK BEST
FOR DAWN AND DUSK.

BLACK AND WHITE

YOUR COMIC STRIP MAY HAVE TO VIE FOR ATTENTION IF THERE ARE OTHER STRIPS ON THE SAME PAGE. TO MAKE YOUR WORK STAND OUT, YOU COULD ADD BLOCKS OF BLACK TO CATCH THE READER'S EYE. HOWEVER, YOU SHOULD NOT OVERDO THIS. THE IDEAL STRATEGY WOULD BE TO ALTERNATE THE BLACK BLOCKS WITH WHITE ONES.

YOU CAN MAKE A STRIP STAND OUT OR INCREASE THE VISUAL CONTRAST OF A FRAME BY USING BLACK AND WHITE. 'ARCHWAY SHADING' IS A POPULAR TECHNIQUE AMONG CARTOONISTS, WHERE AN ARCHWAY IS ADDED TO THE BACKGROUND AND INKED IN BLACK. THIS IS DONE USUALLY WHEN THE BACKGROUND IS EMPTY.

ARCHWAY SHADING BLACK BACKGROUND

YET ANOTHER METHOD IS TO MAKE THE BACKGROUND BLACK. THIS CAN MAKE THE COMPOSITION INSTANTLY DRAMATIC. OF COURSE YOU ARE FREE TO TRY OUT YOUR OWN VARIATIONS.

ALTERNATING BLACK WITH WHITE

TO AVOID OVER-RUNNING YOUR COMIC STRIP WITH BLOCKS OF BLACK, YOU CAN ALTERNATE BLACK WITH WHITE AS SHOWN IN THESE CLOTHING EXAMPLES.

LETTERING BALLOONS

WHETHER YOU TELL YOUR CARTOON STRIP STORY WITH PICTURES OR NOT, LETTERING WILL REMAIN A VERY IMPORTANT PART OF THE EXERCISE. THE SUCCESS OF YOUR COMIC STRIP DEPENDS ON A GOOD, **LEGIBLE LETTERING STYLE** THAT **COMMUNICATES** WELL.

FIRST USE A PENCIL TO DRAW YOUR LETTERS, THEN USE A PEN ENSURING CONSISTENT LINE THICKNESS.

STANDARD BALLOON LETTERING

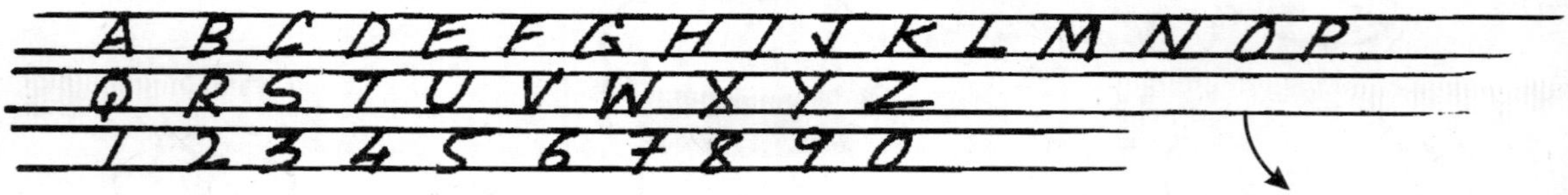

MEASURE AND DRAW TWO EQUIDISTANT HORIZONTAL LINES.

CAPTION LETTERING

THIS IS BY FAR THE MOST COMMONLY USED FORM OF LETTERING. CAPTION LETTERING CAN BE USED WITHIN A SPEECH BALLOON OR UNDER THE RELEVANT FRAME. THE TRADITIONAL METHOD IS TO USE HAND LETTERING. IT IS PREFERRED BY CARTOONISTS WHO WISH TO DEVELOP THEIR OWN STYLE OF LETTERING ACCORDING TO THE MANNER IN WHICH THE COMIC STRIP HAS BEEN DESIGNED ON THE WHOLE.

HOWEVER, THESE DAYS, COMPUTER FONTS ARE ALSO BEING USED. THE FIRST STEP IS TO DRAW TWO PARALLEL GUIDING LINES. PLACE YOUR LETTERS WITHIN THESE LINES IN UPPERCASE. ONCE YOU HAVE FINISHED INKING THE FINAL ARTWORK, YOU SHOULD ERASE THESE GUIDELINES.

HAND-LETTERED CAPTION

COMPUTER FONT LETTERING

SOUND LETTERING

WORDS SUCH AS 'BOOM', 'BLAM' AND 'CRASH' ARE STANDARD IN A COMIC STRIP AND OFTEN A PART OF THE ILLUSTRATION. THEY ARE NOT ADD-ONS.

THESE SOUND EFFECTS ARE ASSOCIATED WITH ACTION. THEY NOT ONLY EMPHASISE WHAT IS GOING ON IN THE PICTURE BUT ALSO ALLOW THE READER TO 'HEAR'.

FIRST STUDY THE ACTION AND THEN GIVE THE WORD THE TREATMENT THAT WILL BEST REFLECT THE ACTION.

USE OF WRITTEN WORDS TO REPRESENT SOUNDS IS CALLED **ONOMATOPOEIA!**

IMPACT LETTERING TAKING UP ALL THE SPACE

SOUND AND PICTURE COMBINED WITH BIG LETTERING

TITLE LETTERING

YOU WILL REALISE THAT IT IS NOT ALWAYS EASY TO COME UP WITH A NAME FOR YOUR COMIC STRIP ON THE BASIS OF YOUR CHARACTER OR THEME. THE TITLE WILL ALSO ENSURE THAT YOU DO NOT DEVIATE FROM THE SCRIPT.

THE TITLE SHOULD BE INSTANTLY RECOGNISABLE BY THE READER AND SHOULD BE SUCH THAT IT CREATES A SENSE OF ANTICIPATION IN THE READER. HOWEVER, THERE IS NO GROUND RULE AS FAR AS THE LETTERING STYLE IS CONCERNED. IT WOULD BE A GOOD IDEA TO BROWSE THE INTERNET AND ENSURE THAT THE TITLE DOESN'T ALREADY EXIST ELSEWHERE.

SPEECH BALLOONS

NOT ALL COMIC STRIPS DEPEND ON WORDS OR DIALOGUES. HOWEVER, SOME ARE MEANT TO BE CONVERSATION PIECES WHERE CHARACTERS SPEAK TO ONE ANOTHER WITHIN THE FRAME. THEIR DIALOGUES ARE ENCLOSED WITHIN WHITE SPACES KNOWN AS SPEECH BALLOONS OR BUBBLES.

CHOOSING A SPEECH BALLOON DEPENDS ON THE NUMBER OF CHARACTERS SPEAKING AND THE SPACE AVAILABLE IN THE FRAME.

CREATE INNOVATIVE SPEECH BALLOONS AND SEE HOW THEY FIT INTO YOUR CARTOON NARRATIVES.

MAKE THE BALLOONS CONFORM TO THE SHAPE OF THE LETTERING.

BEYOND THE BASICS, THERE ARE A FEW ADVANCED TECHNIQUES, LISTED BELOW.

CHARACTERS SPEAKING AT THE SAME TIME

SOME CARTOONISTS DO WITHOUT SPEECH BALLOONS.

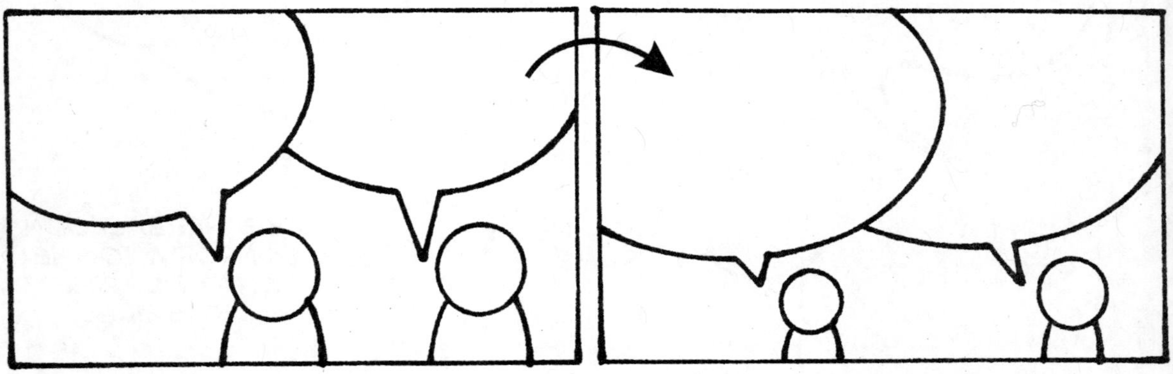

YOU CAN INCREASE THE SIZE OF THE SPEECH BALLOONS BY PUSHING THE CHARACTERS DOWN IN THE FRAME OR MAKING THEM SMALLER.

YOU CAN GET MORE SPACE BY PLACING THE CHARACTER IN FRONT OF THE SPEECH BALLOON.

DON'T LET THE CHARACTER BE PARTLY HIDDEN BY THE SPEECH BALLOON.

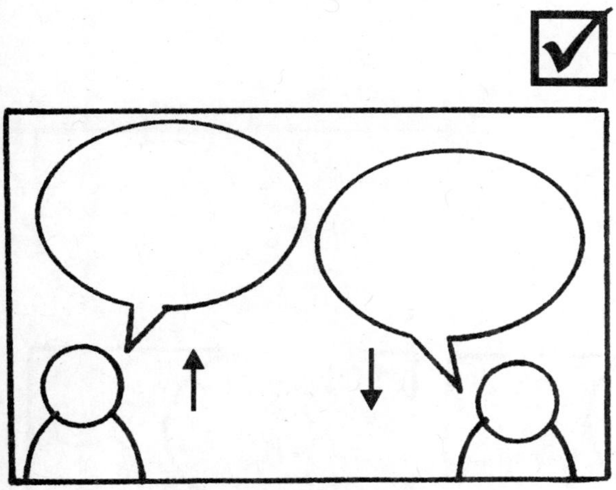

THE SPEECH BALLOON FOR THE CHARACTER WHO SPEAKS FIRST SHOULD BE TO THE LEFT AND THE BALLOON FOR THE CHARACTER SPEAKING SECOND TO THE RIGHT.

AVOID THIS KIND OF CLUMSINESS.

A SPEECH BALLOON TAKES UP A LOT OF SPACE IN THE COMIC STRIP FRAME. FOLLOW THE EXAMPLES BELOW TO CREATE MORE SPACE FOR SPEECH BALLOONS.

TO GET MORE SPACE, **CUT OFF** THE TOP OF THE SPEECH BALLOON.

SOMETIMES YOU CAN 'BREAK THE FRAME', BY TAKING THE SPEECH BALLOON INTO THE NEXT PANEL.

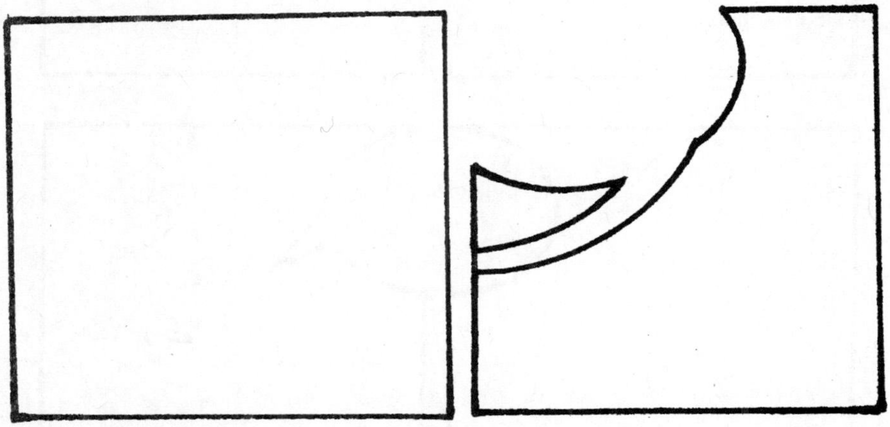

A CUT-OFF BALLOON POINTER SUGGESTS THAT THE CHARACTER IS OUTSIDE THE FRAME.

WHEN A CHARACTER SPEAKS IN THE MIDDLE OF AN ACTION.

WHEN CHARACTERS DO NOT HAVE TO FACE EACH OTHER TO CONVERSE.

OMIT SPEECH BALLOONS FOR NARRATION BETWEEN FRAMES.

MEANTIME MOM DISCUSSES THE BIRTHDAY PLAN...

RECTANGULAR BOXES ARE ALSO USED WITHIN A PANEL FOR NARRATION.

AVOID PUTTING TWO DIFFERENT THOUGHTS OF A CHARACTER IN A SINGLE BALLOON. TWO BALLOONS ARE MORE EFFECTIVE.

TWO OR THREE MORPHED BALLOONS
CAN CREATE AN INTERESTING SHAPE.

SPLASH BALLOON ARE USED
FOR OUTBURSTS.

1. MULTIPLE BALLOONS

THESE SHOW BACK-AND-FORTH CONVERSATIONS.

2. LAYERED BALLOONS

BALLOONS ARE CONNECTED WHEN DIALOGUES ARE LONG.

3. MORPHED BALLOONS

BALLOONS ARE CONNECTED WHEN DIALOGUES ARE LONG.

SPEECH BALLOONS FOR ANIMAL COMIC STRIPS

THERE ARE RULES WHEN IT COMES TO CARTOON ANIMALS TALKING TO ONE ANOTHER, ANIMALS TALK WITH EACH OTHER USING REGULAR SPEECH BALLOONS JUST LIKE HUMAN CHARACTERS.

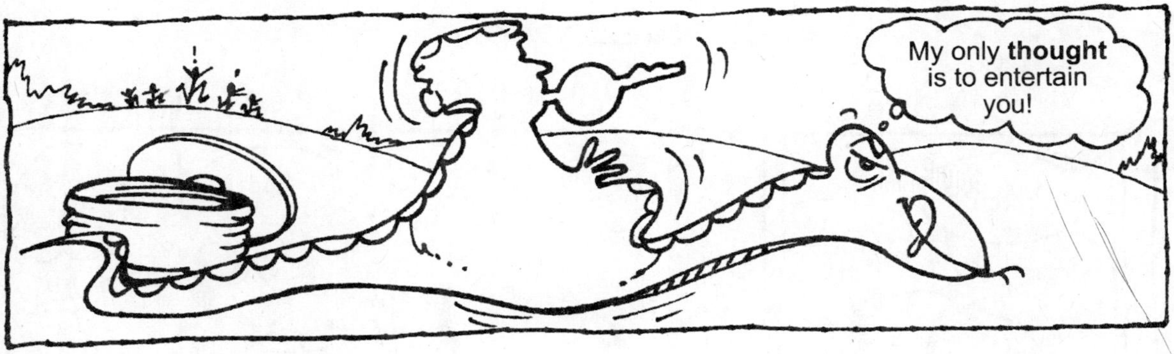

THEY ADDRESS EACH OTHER AND EVEN THE READERS THROUGH THOUGHT BALLOONS. THEY CAN LISTEN TO THE THOUGHT BALLOONS OF OTHER ANIMALS, MAKING THEM APPEAR SMARTER THAN US.

COMIC STRIPS WITH ANIMALS AND PEOPLE

COMIC STRIPS DEPICTING PETS OFTEN SHOW ANIMALS COMMUNICATING WITH PEOPLE IN THE STRIPS THROUGH THOUGHT BALLOONS. THE PEOPLE, ON THE OTHER HAND, SPEAK TO ANIMALS THROUGH REGULAR SPEECH BALLOONS.

THIS IS BECAUSE WHILE THE ANIMALS CAN HEAR WHAT THE PEOPLE SAY, PEOPLE CANNOT HEAR WHAT THE ANIMALS ARE 'THINKING'.

COMIC STRIPS WITH ADULTS AND BABIES

BABIES USE THOUGHT BALLOONS IN THE SAME WAY AS ANIMALS DO WHEN THEY INTERACT WITH PEOPLE. JUST LIKE WITH ANIMALS, ADULTS CANNOT LISTEN TO WHAT BABIES ARE THINKING.

POPULAR PANEL PATTERNS

CERTAIN FEELINGS CAN BE CONVEYED TO THE READER BY THE WAY THE PANEL'S BORDERS ARE DRAWN. THE MOST COMMON PANEL BORDER IS STANDARD RECTANGULAR. A CLOUD-LIKE PANEL BORDER IS USED TO DEPICT WHAT A CHARACTER IS IMAGINING. IT COULD ALSO BE PART OF A CHARACTER'S NARRATIVE. A JAGGED PANEL BORDER IS USED TO CONVEY VIOLENCE, NOISE OR IMPACT. A WAVY PANEL BORDER INDICATES EVENTS IN THE PAST OR FUTURE. EMOTIONAL PEAKS CAN BE SHOWN WITHOUT PANEL BORDERS. NOVEL PANEL BORDERS CAN ALSO BE DRAWN IN THE FORM OF WINDOWS, DOORS, CAVE MOUTH OR HUMAN EYES. CHARACTERS CAN BE MADE TO OVERLAP PANEL BOUNDARIES FOR MORE IMPACT AND MOTION TOWARDS THE READER.

YOU CAN EVEN SKIP A PANEL AND LEAVE THE PICTURE STANDING FREE.

SEPARATING PANEL

IF THERE IS NO CHANGE IN THE LOCATION OR THE TIME, YOU NEED NOT DIVIDE THE PANELS AT ALL. READERS WILL FOLLOW THE SEQUENCE. THE CARTOON STRIP WILL STAND OUT AMIDST OTHER DAILY STRIPS BECAUSE OF THIS **OPENNESS**.

BREAKTHROUGH PANEL

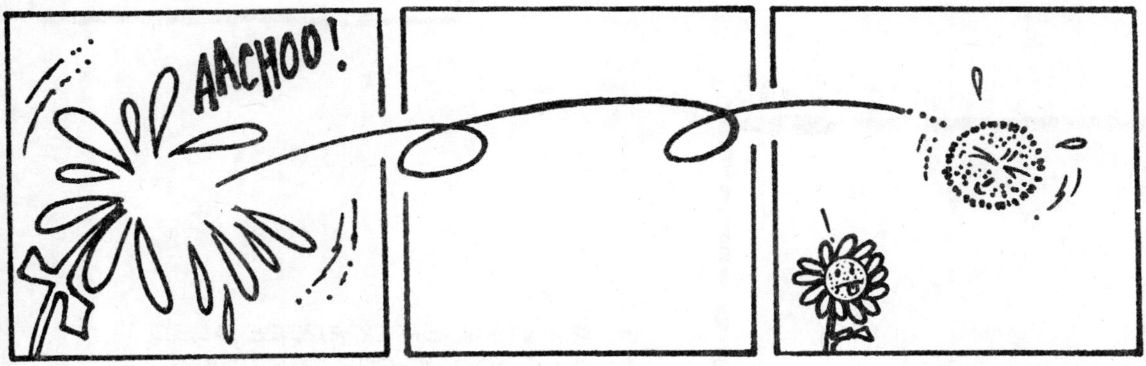

A POPULAR DEVICE USED TO DEPICT RAPID MOVEMENT IS BY BREAKING THROUGH PANELS.

COMIC FRAME SAMPLES

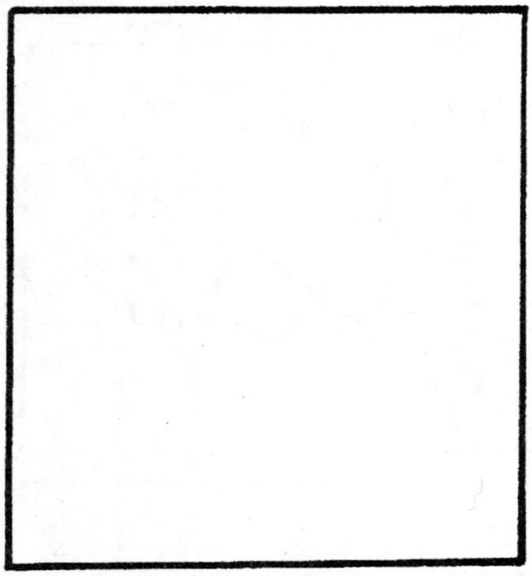

1. PANELS WITH RULED BORDERS LOOK NEAT.

2. FREEHAND BORDERS ARE ALSO POPULAR. TO KEEP THEM STRAIGHT, DRAW RULED LINES IN PENCIL AND INK THEM WITH A PEN.

3. PAINTBRUSH BORDERS ALSO LOOK GOOD WHERE THE LINES VARY SLIGHTLY IN THICKNESS.

POPULAR ALTERNATIVE COMIC PANEL

RECTANGULAR PANEL WITH
CURVED CORNERS

SOUND EFFECT PANELS

A PANEL TAKEN UP ENTIRELY BY A SOUND EFFECT, SUCH AS 'THUD' OR 'BANG', IS GOOD FOR PACING THE STORYLINE. CAPITAL LETTERING IS PREFERRED FOR EMPHASIS.

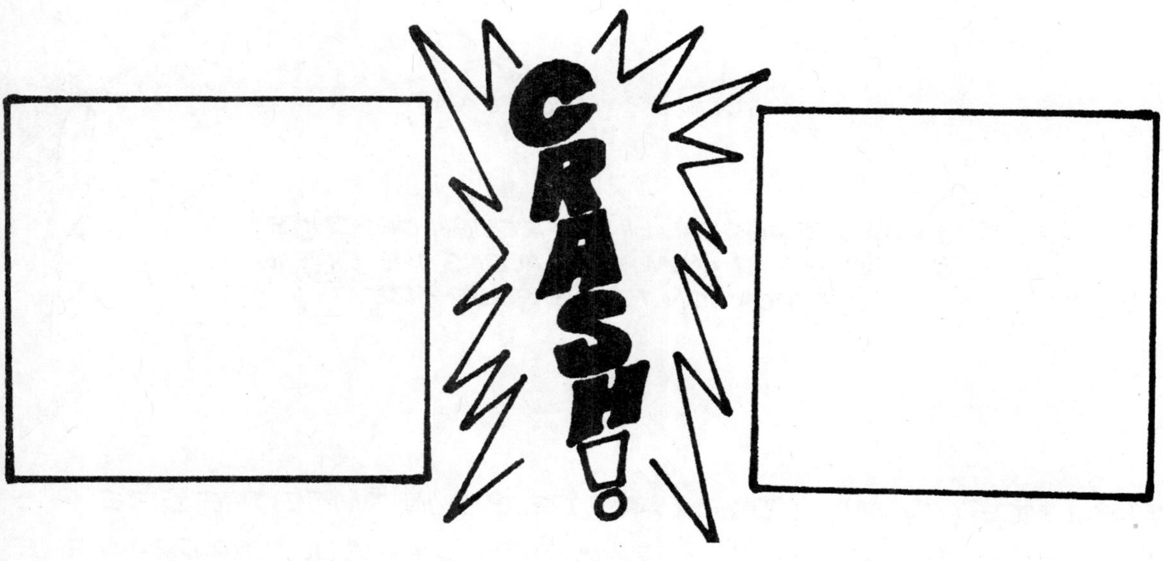

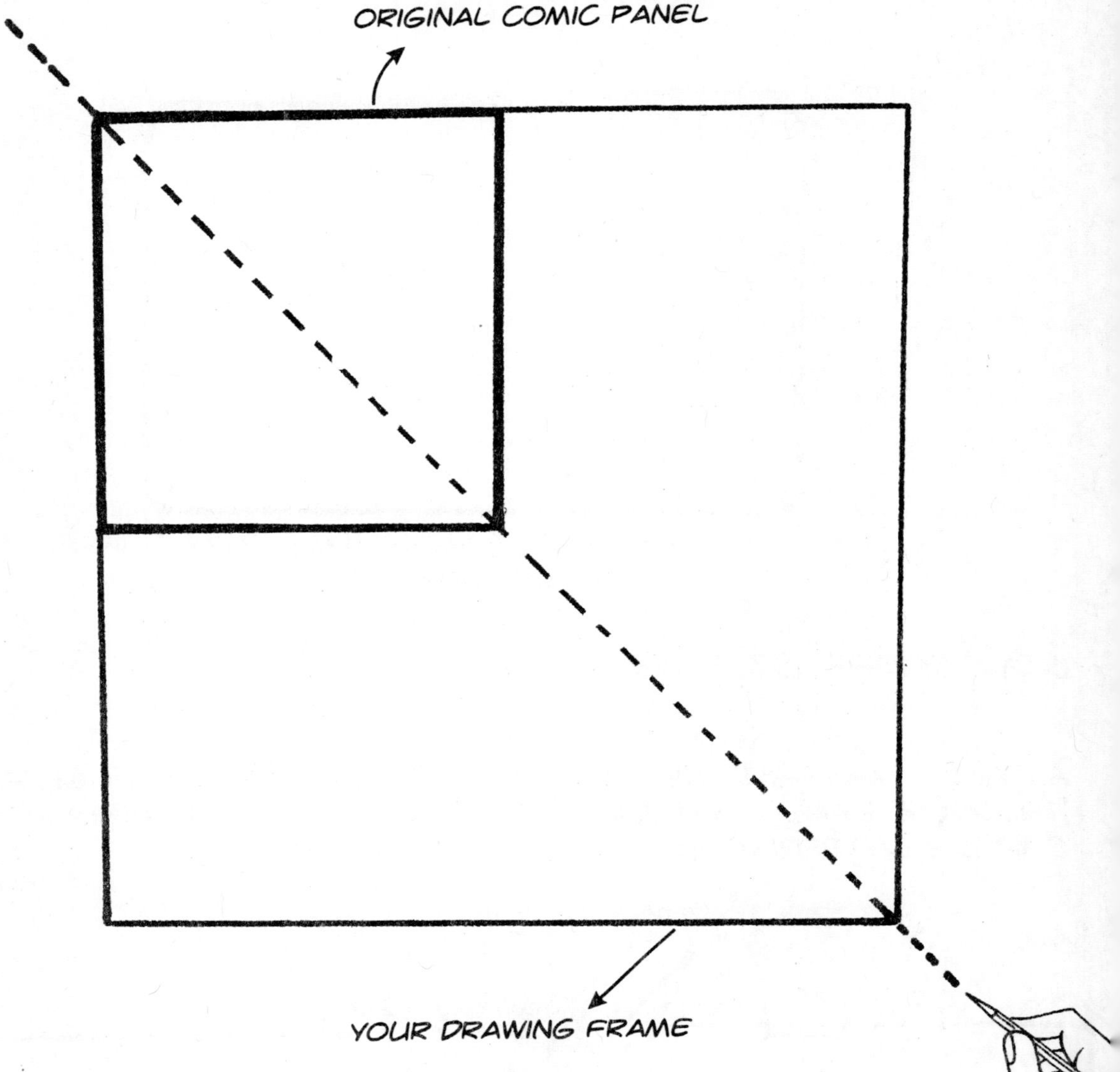

DRAW A DIAGONAL LINE THROUGH OPPOSITE CORNERS AND ANYWHERE ALONG THE LINE IN PROPORTION TO THE FIXED SIZE.

TIP : MOST COMIC STRIPS ARE DRAWN IN TWICE THE SIZE THEY ARE PRINTED IN, OTHERWISE IT'S DIFFICULT TO DRAW THE DETAILS AND PUT IN LEGIBLE LETTERING IN EACH PANEL.

POPULAR PANEL VARIATIONS FOR A DAILY COMIC STRIP

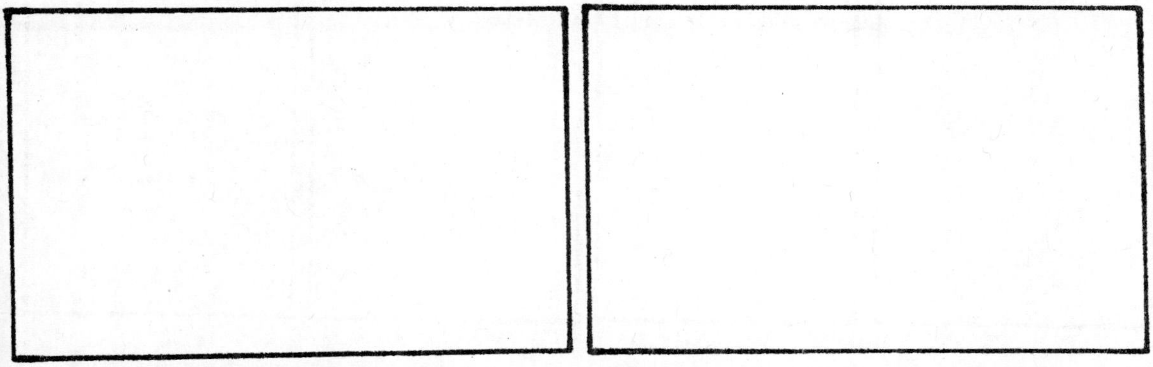

VARIETY

NEWSPAPER STYLE THREE-PANEL SETUP

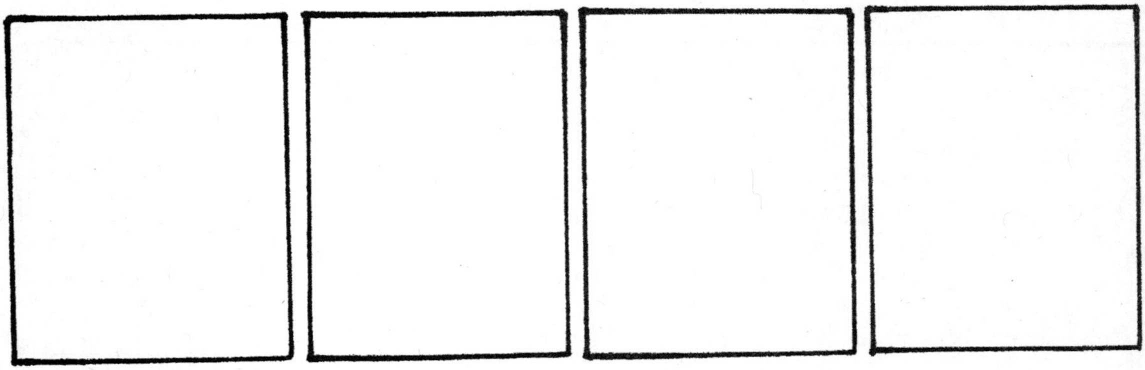

TRADITIONAL FOUR-PANEL SETUP

SECOND PANEL USED FOR SOUND EFFECT OR CLOSE-UP SHOT

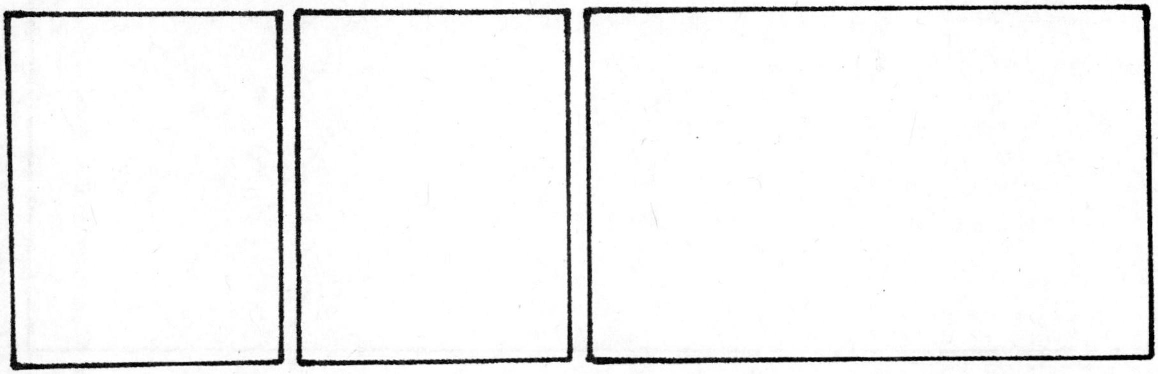

PANELS BUILDING UP TO A BIG PUNCHLINE SCENE

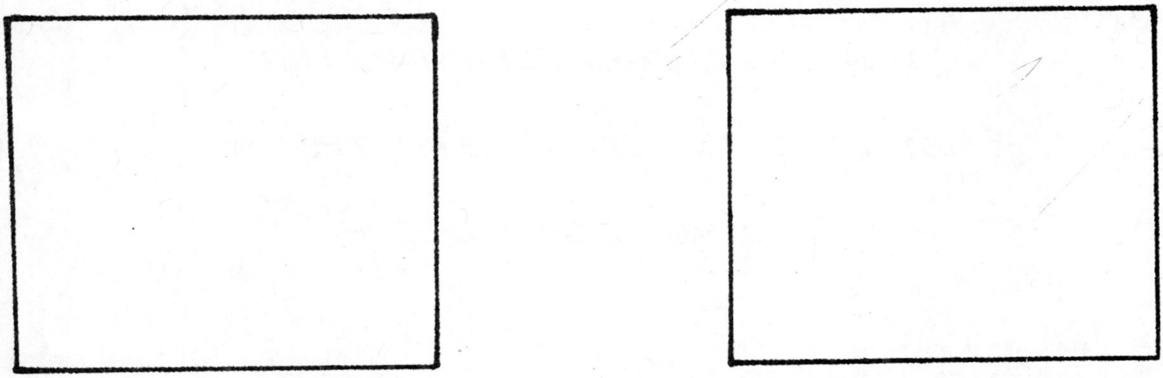

BORDERLESS MIDDLE PANEL

LONG STRIP FOR VISUAL GAG

AS LONG AS YOUR COMIC STRIP PANELS ARE EQUAL IN SHAPE AND SIZE, YOU CAN DRAW THE FRAMES IN ANY DIMENSION YOU LIKE.

I HOPE THIS BOOK HAS INSPIRED AND ENCOURAGED YOU TO GRAB A PAPER AND PENCIL TO CREATE YOUR FIRST ORIGINAL COMIC STRIP.

HAPPY CARTOONING!

Other books by the author

How To Draw Animal Cartoons

Ajit Narayan

Handy tips from an experienced cartoonist.

ISBN: 9788176559676
Pages: 76
Format: PB

Cartooning with Ajit Naraya

Ajit Narayan
Layout design: Rima Kaushik

Simple steps that teach cartooning techniques.

ISBN: 9788176554545
Pages: 60
Format: PB

Draw Cartoons with

Ajit Narayan

Ajit Narayan shares his skills to help you master one of the most popular art forms of our times.

ISBN: 9788176558557
Pages: 80
Format: PB